To Mum
Lots of L
Marian
and
Fami
(ch ... gary

The large print Prayer Book

Favourite prayers, poems and Bible readings

kevin mayhew

kevin mayhew

First published in Great Britain in 2009 by Kevin Mayhew Ltd
Buxhall, Stowmarket, Suffolk IP14 3BW
Tel: +44 (0) 1449 737978 Fax: +44 (0) 1449 737834
E-mail: info@kevinmayhewltd.com

www.kevinmayhew.com

9 8 7 6 5 4 3 2 1

ISBN 978 1 84867 154 6
Catalogue No. 1501175

Cover design by Rob Mortonson
Typeset by Rob Mortonson

Printed and bound in Great Britain

Contents

Prayers for lifestyle

Prayers for individuals and families

Blessings

Traditional prayers

The Lord's Prayer

Our Father, who art in heaven,
hallowed be thy name.
Thy Kingdom come, thy will be done,
on earth as it is in heaven.

Give us this day our daily bread;
and forgive us our trespasses,
as we forgive those who
trespass against us.

And lead us not into temptation,
but deliver us from evil.
For thine is the Kingdom,
the Power and the Glory,
For ever and ever.

Gloria

Glory to the Father and to the Son
and to the Holy Spirit:
as it was in the beginning, is now
and shall be for ever.
Amen.

Prayers of love and peace

Never too busy to care

Lord, make me so sensitive
to the needs of those around me
that I never fail to know
when they're hurting or afraid;
or when they're simply crying out
for someone's touch to ease their loneliness.
Let me love so much that my
first thought is of others
and my last thought is of me.

Michael Forster

Love one another

I give you a new commandment,
that you love one another.
Just as I have loved you,
you also should love one another.
By this everyone will know that
you are my disciples,
if you have love for one another.

John 13:34, 35

Goodness is stronger than evil

Goodness is stronger than evil;
love is stronger than hate;
light is stronger than darkness;
life is stronger than death;
victory is ours through him who loves us.

Desmond Tutu, An African Prayer Book (1995)

I said a prayer

I said a prayer for you today
and know God must have heard –
I felt the answer in my heart
although he spoke no word!
I didn't ask for wealth or fame
(I knew you wouldn't mind) –
I asked him to send treasures
of a far more lasting kind!

I asked that he'd be near you
at the start of each new day
to grant you health and blessings
and friends to share your way!

I asked for happiness for you
in all things great and small –
but it was for his loving care
I prayed the most of all!

Frank J. Zamboni

Love

Love is patient; love is kind;
love is not envious or boastful
or arrogant or rude.
It does not insist on its own way;
it is not irritable or resentful;
it does not rejoice in wrongdoing,
but rejoices in the truth.
It bears all things,
believes all things,
hopes all things,
endures all things.
Love never ends.

1 Corinthians 13:4-8

Set my heart on fire

Set my heart on fire
with love for you, O Christ,
that in its flame I may love you
with all my heart,
and with all my mind,
with all my soul
and with all my strength,
and my neighbour as myself,
so that keeping your commandments,
I may glorify you,
the giver of all good gifts.

Kontakion for Love, Eastern Orthodox

Everlasting love

I love you
with an everlasting love.

Jeremiah 31:3
(Version unknown)

A prayer of compassion

Watch, dear Lord,
with those who wake, or watch,
or weep tonight,
and give your angels charge
over those who sleep.
Tend your sick ones, O Lord Christ,
rest your weary ones,
bless your dying ones,
soothe your suffering ones,
pity your afflicted ones,
shield your joyous ones.
I ask all this for your love's sake.

St Augustine of Hippo (354–430)

Love is from God

Beloved, let us love one another,
because love is from God;
everyone who loves
is born of God and knows God.
Whoever does not love does not know God,
for God is love.

1 John 4:7, 8

Friendship

A friend is like a tower strong;
a friend is like the joyous song
that helps us on our way.
When golden ties of friendship bind
the heart to heart, the mind to mind
how fortunate are we!

For friendship is a noble thing;
it soars past death on angel's wing
into eternity.
God blesses friendship's holy bond
both here and in the great beyond:
a benefit unpriced.

Then may we know that wondrous joy,
that precious ore without alloy;
a friendship based on Christ.

Someone who cares

Lord, make my heart a haven
where the lonely may find friendship,
where the weary may find shelter,
where the helpless may find refuge,
where the hopeless may find hope,
where all those who seek someone who cares
may enter and find you.

Peace

Lead me from death to life,
from falsehood to truth;
lead me from despair to hope,
from fear to trust.

Lead me from hate to love,
from war to peace;
let your peace fill my heart,
my life and my world.

Satish Kumar, from The Upanishads (c. 9th century)

Prayers of trust, hope and rest

I am with you always

I am with you in the springtime
of your life, when joy is new,
and when the summer brings the
fullness of your faith,
I'm there with you.
I am with you in the autumn
of your years, to turn to gold
every memory of your yesterdays,
to banish winter's cold.
I am with you in the sunshine,
when your world glows warm and bright.
I am with you when life's shadows
bring long hours of endless night.
I am with you every moment,
every hour of every day –
go in peace upon life's journey,
for I'm with you all the way.

I will give you rest

Come to me, all you that are weary
and are carrying heavy burdens,
and I will give you rest.
Take my yoke upon you, and learn from me;
for I am gentle and humble in heart,
and you will find rest for your souls.
For my yoke is easy, and my burden is light.

Matthew 11:28-30

God has not promised

God has not promised
sun without rain,
joy without sorrow,
peace without pain.
But God has promised
strength for the day,
rest for the labour,
light for the way,
grace for the trials,
help from above,
unfailing sympathy,
undying love.

Annie Johnson Flint (1919)

The Lord our protector

I lift my eyes to the hills.
From whence does my help come?
My help comes from the Lord,
who made heaven and earth.

He will not let your foot be moved,
he who keeps you will not slumber.
Behold, he who keeps Israel
will neither slumber nor sleep.

The Lord is your keeper;
the Lord is your shade on your right hand.
The sun shall not smite you by day,
nor the moon by night.

The Lord will keep you from all evil;
he will keep your life.
The Lord will keep your going out and
your coming in,
from this time forth
and for evermore.

Psalm 121 (Version unknown)

Wings of faith

Give us, Lord, a special faith,
unlimited and free,
a faith that isn't bound
by what we know or what we see.

A faith that trusts the sunshine
even when there is no light,
a faith that hears the morning song's
soft echo in the night.

A faith that somehow rises
past unhappiness or pain,
knowing that in every loss
your goodness will remain.

A faith that finds your steadfast love
sufficient for all things,
a faith that lifts the heart above
and gives the spirit wings.

B. J. Holt

Christ be with me

Christ be with me,
Christ within me,
Christ behind me,
Christ before me,
Christ beside me,
Christ to win me,
Christ to comfort
and restore me.

Christ beneath me,
Christ above me,
Christ in quiet,
Christ in danger,
Christ in hearts
of all that love me,
Christ in mouth
of friend and stranger.

St Patrick

At the ending of this day

O Lord my God,
I thank you at the ending of this day.
I thank you for rest of body and mind.
Your hand has been over me,
guarding and preserving me.
Forgive all my littleness of faith
and all the wrong I have done this day,
and help me to forgive all
who have done wrong to me.
Let me sleep in peace under your care.
I commit to you all whom I love,
all in this house,
and myself, both body and soul.
O God, praise be to your holy name.

Guard me while I sleep

Save me, O Lord, while I am awake,
and guard me while I sleep,
that awake I may watch with Christ,
and asleep I may rest in peace,
in Jesus' name.

The Office of Compline

Safe through the night

Now I lay me down to sleep
I pray the Lord my soul to keep,
and keep me safe throughout the night,
and wake me with the morning light.

Prayers of thanksgiving

Prayer of Richard of Chichester

Thanks be to you
my Lord Jesus Christ,
for all the benefits which
you have given me;
for all the pains and insults
which you have borne for me,
O most merciful Redeemer,
Friend, and Brother.
May I know you more clearly,
love you more dearly
and follow you more nearly.

A thankful song

To God who gives our daily bread
a thankful song we raise,
and pray that he who sends us food
may fill our hearts with praise.

Thomas Tallis (1510-1585)

Grateful thanks

O eternal God,
helper of the helpless,
comforter of the comfortless,
hope of the afflicted,
bread of the hungry,
drink of the thirsty,
and saviour of all who wait upon you:
I bless and glorify your name;
I adore your goodness and delight in your love.
Take from me every tendency
toward sin or vanity;
let my desires soar upwards to your love,
that I may hunger and thirst
for the bread of life
and the wine of heaven,
and know no love but yours.

Jeremy Taylor (1613–1667)

Prayers for sorrow and anxiety

Life's journey

The road of life may take us
where we do not care to go;
up rocky paths, down darkened trails,
our steps unsure and slow.
But our dear Lord extends his hands
to hold, to help, to guide us;
we never have to feel alone
for he walks close beside us.

The Difference

I got up early one morning and
rushed right into the day;
I had so much to accomplish
that I didn't have time to pray.
Problems just tumbled about me,
and heavier came each task.
'Why doesn't God help me?'
I wondered;
he answered, 'You didn't ask.'

I wanted to see joy and beauty,
but the day toiled on grey and bleak;
I wondered why God didn't show me;
he said, 'You didn't seek.'
I tried to come into God's presence;
I used all my keys to the lock.
God gently and lovingly chided,
'My child, you didn't knock.'

I woke early this morning
and paused before entering the day;
I had so much to accomplish
that I had to take time to pray.

Footprints

One night I had a dream.
I dreamed I was walking along
the beach with God,
and across the sky flashed
scenes from my life. For each scene
I noticed two sets of footprints
in the sand, one belonged to me
and the other to God.
When the last scene of my life
flashed before me I looked back at
the footprints in the sand. I noticed
that at times along the path of life
there was only one set of footprints.

I also noticed that it happened at
the very lowest and saddest times
of my life. This really bothered me
and I questioned God about it.
'God, you said that once I decided
to follow you, you would walk
with me all the way, but I noticed
that during the most troublesome
times in my life there is only one

Continued overleaf

set of footprints. I don't understand
why in times when I needed you
most, you would leave me.'

God replied, 'My precious, precious child,
I love you and I would never, never
leave you during your times of
trials and suffering.
When you see only one set of footprints
it was then that I carried you.'

Mary Stevenson

Take courage!

I can't change what you're going through,
I have no words to make a difference;
no answers or solutions
to make things easier for you.

But if it helps in any way,
I want to say I care.

Please know that even when you're lonely,
you're not alone.

I'll be here,
supporting you with all my thoughts,
cheering for you with all my strength,
praying for you with all my heart.

For whatever you need,
for as long as it takes –

lean on my love.

Do not worry

Do not worry about anything,
but in everything
by prayer and supplication with thanksgiving
let your requests be made known to God.
And the peace of God,
which surpasses all understanding,
will guard your hearts
and your minds in Christ Jesus.

Philippians 4:6, 7

What is dying?

A ship sails and I stand watching
till she fades on the horizon
and someone at my side says,
'She is gone.'
Gone where?
Gone from my sight, that is all;
she is just as large
as when I saw her.
The diminished size
and total loss of sight
is in me, not in her;
and just at that moment
when someone at my side says,
'She is gone',
there are others
who are watching her coming
and other voices
take up a glad shout,
'There she comes!'
And that is dying.

Bishop Charles H. Brent

Death is nothing at all

Death is nothing at all.
I have only slipped away into the next room.
I am I, and you are you.
Whatever we were to each other,
that we still are.

Call me by my old familiar name,
speak to me in the easy way
which you always used.

Put no difference in your tone,
wear no forced air of solemnity or sorrow.
Laugh as we always laughed
at the little jokes we enjoyed together.

Let my name be ever the household word
that it always was,
let it be spoken without effect,
without the trace of a shadow on it.

Life means all that it ever meant.
It is the same as it ever was;
there is unbroken continuity.

Continued overleaf

Why should I be out of mind
because I am out of sight?

I am waiting for you,
for an interval,
somewhere very near,
just around the corner.

All is well.

Henry Scott Holland

Hold my hand

Hold my hand, Lord.
Walk me through the loneliness
and the valley of my sorrow.
Hold onto me when I'm too afraid
to think about tomorrow.
Let me lean on you, Lord,
when I'm too weary to go on.
Hold my hand, Lord, through the night
until I see the light of dawn.

The twenty-third Psalm

The Lord is my shepherd, I shall not want.
He makes me lie down in green pastures;
he leads me beside still waters;
he restores my soul.
He leads me in right paths for his name's sake.

Even though I walk through the darkest valley,
I fear no evil;
for you are with me;
your rod and your staff – they comfort me.

You prepare a table before me
in the presence of my enemies;
you anoint my head with oil;
my cup overflows.
Surely goodness and mercy shall follow me
all the days of my life,
and I shall dwell in the house of the Lord
my whole life long.

Those who live in the Lord

Those who live in the Lord never
see each other for the last time.

German Proverb

For God so loved the world

For God so loved the world
that he gave his only Son,
so that everyone who believes in him
may not perish but may have eternal life.

John 3:16

Life Eternal

I am the resurrection and the life.
Those who believe in me,
even though they die, will live,
and everyone who lives and believes in me
will never die.

John 11:25, 26

Prayers for forgiveness

Forgive me my sins

Forgive me my sins, O Lord;
forgive me the sins of my youth
and the sins of my age,
the sins of my soul and the sins of my body,
my secret and my whispering sins,
my presumptuous and my crying sins,
the sins I have done to please myself,
and the sins I have done to please others.
Forgive me the sins which I know,
and those sins which I know not;
forgive them, O Lord,
forgive them all of thy great goodness.

Lancelot Andrewes (1555-1626)

Deliver me from sin

Lord our God,
grant me grace to desire you
with my whole heart;
that so desiring you, I may seek and find you;
and so finding you, I may love you;
and so loving you, I may hate those sins
from which you have delivered me,
through Jesus Christ our Lord.

St Anselm (1033-1109)

Have mercy upon me

May Almighty God have mercy upon me,
forgive me my sins
and bring me to eternal life,
through Jesus Christ our Lord.

Prayers for lifestyle

Prayer for serenity

God grant me
the serenity to accept
the things I cannot change,
the courage to change the things I can,
and wisdom to know the difference.

Reinhold Niebuhr (1892–1971)

The cross in my pocket

I carry a cross in my pocket;
a simple reminder to me
of the fact that I am a Christian
no matter where I may be.
This little cross is not magic,
nor is it a good-luck charm.
It isn't meant to protect me
from every physical harm.
It's not for identification
for all the world to see.
It's simply an understanding
between my Saviour and me.

Continued overleaf

When I put my hand in my pocket
to bring out a coin or a key,
the cross is there to remind me
of the price he paid for me.
It reminds me, too, to be thankful
for my blessings day by day,
and to strive to serve him better
in all that I do and say.
It's also a daily reminder
of the peace and comfort I share
with all who know my Master
and give themselves to his care.
So, I carry a cross in my pocket
reminding no one but me
that Jesus Christ, is the Lord of my life,
if only I'll let him be.

Norma Thomas

Take time

Take time to THINK . . .
it is the source of power.
Take time to PLAY . . .
it is the secret of perpetual youth.

Take time to READ . . .
it is the fountain of wisdom.
Take time to PRAY . . .
it is the greatest power on earth.
Take time to LOVE and BE LOVED . . .
it is a God-given privilege.

Take time to BE FRIENDLY . . .
it is the road to happiness.
Take time to LAUGH . . .
it is the music of the soul.
Take time to GIVE . . .
it is too short a day to be selfish.
Take time to WORK . . .
it is the price of success.
Take time to DO CHARITY . . .
it is the key to heaven.

Be still

Be still, and know
that I am God.

Psalm 46:10
(Version unknown)

Prayer of Dedication

Lord Jesus,
I give you my hands to do your work.
I give you my feet to go your way.
I give you my eyes to see as you do.
I give you my tongue to speak your words.
I give you my mind that you may think in me.
I give you my spirit that you may pray in me.
Above all, I give you my heart
that you may love in me.
I give you my whole self
that you may grow in me,
so that it is you, Lord Jesus,
who lives and works
and prays in me.

Lancelot Andrewes (1555–1626)

The right attitude

Teach me, good Lord,
not to complain about excessive work
or shortness of time;
not to exaggerate the tasks I undertake
by pretending to be burdened by them;
but to accept them all in freedom and joy.
Teach me not to call attention to busyness
or petty irritations;
not to become so dependent upon others'
appreciation of me
that my motives become suspect;
not to demand respect from other people
merely on account of my age
or past achievements.

Edward Benson (1829–1896)

Serving God

Help me, O God,
to serve you and your world well today.
May I do my work carefully,
help others without indulging in ostentation,
enjoy your gifts of food and drink,
but without vulgarity or excess,
and be a good friend to others.
Then may I go to bed contented
and sleep well,
through Jesus Christ my Lord.

Based on a medieval prayer

The Beatitudes

Blessed are the poor in spirit,
for theirs is the kingdom of heaven.
Blessed are those who mourn,
for they will be comforted.
Blessed are the meek,
for they will inherit the earth.
Blessed are those who hunger and thirst for righteousness, for they will be filled.
Blessed are the merciful,
for they will receive mercy.
Blessed are the pure in heart,
for they will see God.
Blessed are the peacemakers,
for they will be called children of God.
Blessed are those who are persecuted for righteousness' sake,
for theirs is the kingdom of heaven.
Blessed are you when people revile you and persecute you and utter all kinds of evil against you falsely on my account.
Rejoice and be glad, for your reward is great in heaven, for in the same way they persecuted the prophets who were before you.

Matthew 5:3-12

As I grow old

Lord, you know better than I know myself
that I am growing older
and will someday be old.
Keep me from the fatal habit
of thinking I must say something
on every subject and on every occasion.

Release me from craving to straighten out
everybody's affairs.
Make me thoughtful but not moody;
helpful but not bossy.
With my vast store of wisdom,
it seems a pity not to use it all,
but you know, Lord,
that I want a few friends at the end.

Keep my mind free
from the recital of endless details;
give me wings to get to the point.
Seal my lips on my aches and pains;
they are increasing,
and love of rehearsing them
is becoming sweeter as the years go by.

I dare not ask for grace enough to enjoy
the tales of others' pains,
but help me to endure them with patience.

I dare not ask for improved memory,
but for a growing humility
and a lessening cocksureness
when my memory seems to clash
with the memories of others.
Teach me the glorious lesson that occasionally
I may be mistaken.

Keep me reasonably sweet.
I do not want to be a saint –
some of them are so hard to live with –
but a sour old person
is no great companion, either.

Give me the ability to see good things
in unexpected places,
and talents in unexpected people.
And give me, O Lord,
the grace to tell them so.

Seventeenth century nun's prayer

The prayer of St Augustine of Hippo

Eternal God,
the light of the mind that knows you,
the joy of the heart that loves you,
the strength of the will that serves you;
grant me so to know you
that I may truly love you,
so to love you that I may freely serve you,
to the glory of your holy name.

St Augustine of Hippo (354-430)

God be in my head

God be in my head, and in my understanding.
God be in my eyes, and in my looking.
God be in my mouth, and in my speaking.
God be in my heart, and in my thinking.
God be at my end, and at my departing.

Book of Hours (1514)

Prayers for individuals and families

A prayer for those who live alone

I live alone, dear Lord,
stay by my side;
in all my daily needs
be thou my guide.
Grant me good health,
for that indeed I pray,
to carry on my work
from day to day.

Keep pure my mind,
my thoughts, my every deed,
let me be kind, unselfish,
in my neighbour's need.
Spare me from fire, from flood,
malicious tongues,
from thieves, from fear
and evil ones.

If sickness or an accident befall,
then humbly, Lord, I pray,
hear thou my call.

Continued overleaf

And when I'm feeling low,
or in despair,
lift up my heart
and help me in my prayer.

I live alone, dear Lord,
yet have no fear,
because I feel your presence
ever near.

Marriage prayer

Lord, help us to remember
when we first met
and the strong love
that grew between us;
to work that love
into practical things
so nothing can divide us.
We ask for words
both kind and loving,

and hearts always ready
to ask for forgiveness
as well as to forgive.
Dear Lord,
we put our marriage
into your hands.

Affirm our love

May God, who brought
the two of us together
and joined us as husband and wife,
affirm our love and make us one for ever,
blessing us with joy each day of our life.

Guide for a loving home

May we treat one another
with respect, honesty and care.
May we share the little discoveries
and changes each day brings.

Continued overleaf

May we try always to be sensitive
to one another's joys, sorrows,
needs and changing moods,
and realise that being a loving family
means sometimes not understanding
everyone all the time
but being there to love
and help them just the same.

Bless our home

Bless our home, Father,
that we cherish the bread
before there is none,
discover each other
before we leave,
and enjoy each other
for what we are,
while we have time.

Richard Wong

Be present at our table, Lord

Be present at our table, Lord;
be here and everywhere adored.
Thy creatures bless, and grant that we
may feast in paradise with thee.

John Wesley (1703-1791)

A grace

Bless, O Lord, this food to our use
and our lives in your service,
and make us mindful of the needs of others.

Traditional

Blessings

'God bless you'

How sweetly fall those simple words
upon the human heart;
when friends in holiest terms thus seek
their best wish to impart.
From far or near, they ever seem
to bear a power to cheer you;
and soul responsive beats to soul
in breathing out,
'God bless you'.

A blessing from the Book of Cerne

May God the Father bless us;
may Christ take care of us;
the Holy Spirit enlighten us
all the days of our life,
the Lord be our defender
and keeper of body and soul,
both now and for ever, to the ages of ages.

Book of Cerne (Tenth century)

A blessing

The Lord bless you and keep you;
the Lord make his face to shine upon you,
and be gracious to you;
the Lord lift up his countenance upon you,
and give you peace.

Numbers 6:24-26

Paul's farewell

Be happy
and grow in Christ.
Do what I have said,
and live in harmony
and peace.
May the grace of our Lord
Jesus Christ
be with you all.
May God's love,
and the Holy Spirit's
friendship
be yours.

2 Corinthians 13:11-14

(Version unknown)

Deep peace

Deep peace of the running wave to you.
Deep peace of the flowing air to you.
Deep peace of the quiet earth to you.
Deep peace of the shining stars to you.
Deep peace of the Son of Peace to you.

Celtic Benediction

For the Church

Be mindful of your Church, O Lord.
Deliver it from all evil,
perfect it with your love,
sanctify it,
and gather it together
from throughout the world
into the kingdom
which you have prepared for it.
For yours is the power and the glory
for ever and ever.

The Didache

The Grace

The grace of our Lord Jesus Christ,
the love of God
and the fellowship of the Holy Spirit
be with us all always.

2 Corinthians 13:13
(Version unknown)

His love

May his love enfold you.
May his peace surround you.
May his light touch you.

Favourite Bible readings

Joshua 1:9

I hereby command you:
Be strong and courageous;
do not be frightened or dismayed,
for the Lord your God is with you
wherever you go.

Psalm 51:1, 2

Have mercy on me, O God,
according to your steadfast love;
according to your abundant mercy
blot out my transgressions.
Wash me thoroughly from my iniquity,
and cleanse me from my sin.

Psalm 103:1-4

Bless the Lord, O my soul,
and all that is within me, bless his holy name.
Bless the Lord, O my soul,
and do not forget all his benefits –
who forgives all your iniquity,
who heals all your diseases,
who redeems your life from the Pit,
who crowns you with steadfast love and mercy.

Psalm 129

'Often have they attacked me
from my youth' –
let Israel now say –
'often have they attacked me from my youth,
yet they have not prevailed against me.
The plowers plowed on my back;
they made their furrows long.'
The Lord is righteous;
he has cut the cords of the wicked.

May all who hate Zion
be put to shame and turned backward.
Let them be like the grass on the housetops
that withers before it grows up,
with which reapers do not fill their hands
or binders of sheaves their arms,
while those who pass by do not say,
'The blessing of the Lord be upon you!
We bless you in the name of the Lord!'

Isaiah 25:6-9

On this mountain the Lord of hosts
will make for all peoples
a feast of rich food,
a feast of well-aged wines,
of rich food filled with marrow,
of well-aged wines strained clear.
And he will destroy on this mountain
the shroud that is cast over all peoples,
the sheet that is spread over all nations;
he will swallow up death forever.

Continued overleaf

Then the Lord God will wipe away the tears
from all faces,
and the disgrace of his people
he will take away from all the earth,
for the Lord has spoken.
It will be said on that day,
Lo, this is our God; we have waited for him,
so that he might save us.
This is the Lord for whom we have waited;
let us be glad and rejoice in his salvation.

Isaiah 43:1-4

But now thus says the Lord,
he who created you, O Jacob,
he who formed you, O Israel:
Do not fear, for I have redeemed you;
I have called you by name, you are mine.
When you pass through the waters,
I will be with you;
and through the rivers,
they shall not overwhelm you;

when you walk through fire
you shall not be burned,
and the flame shall not consume you.
For I am the Lord your God,
the Holy One of Israel, your Saviour.
I give Egypt as your ransom,
Ethiopia and Seba in exchange for you.
Because you are precious in my sight,
and honoured, and I love you,
I give people in return for you,
nations in exchange for your life.

Matthew 10:31

So do not be afraid;
you are of more value than many sparrows.

Luke 1:46-55 – The Magnificat

My soul magnifies the Lord,
and my spirit rejoices in God my Saviour,
for he has looked with favour
on the lowliness of his servant.
Surely, from now on
all generations will call me blessed;
for the Mighty One
has done great things for me,
and holy is his name.
His mercy is for those who fear him
from generation to generation.
He has shown strength with his arm;
he has scattered the proud
in the thoughts of their hearts.
He has brought down the powerful
from their thrones,
and lifted up the lowly;
he has filled the hungry with good things,
and sent the rich away empty.
He has helped his servant Israel,
in remembrance of his mercy,
according to the promise
he made to our ancestors,
to Abraham and to his descendants forever.

Luke 2:29-32

Master, now you are dismissing
your servant in peace,
according to your word;
for my eyes have seen your salvation,
which you have prepared
in the presence of all peoples,
a light for revelation to the Gentiles
and for glory to your people Israel.

John 14:1-6

Do not let your hearts be troubled.
Believe in God, believe also in me.
In my Father’s house
there are many dwelling places.
If it were not so, would I have told you
that I go to prepare a place for you?
And if I go and prepare a place for you,
I will come again
and will take you to myself,
so that where I am,
there you may be also.
And you know the way
to the place where I am going.

Continued overleaf

Thomas said to him
'Lord, we do not know where you are going.
How can we know the way?'

Jesus said to him, 'I am the way,
and the truth, and the life.
No one comes to the Father
except through me.'

2 Corinthians 13:11-12

Finally, brothers and sisters, farewell.
Put things in order, listen to my appeal,
agree with one another, live in peace;
and the God of love and peace
will be with you.
Greet one another with a holy kiss.
All the saints greet you.

Galatians 5:22-23

By contrast, the fruit of the Spirit is love,
joy, peace, patience, kindness, generosity,
faithfulness, gentleness, and self-control.
There is no law against such things.

1 Thessalonians 4:13-18

But we do not want you to be uninformed,
brothers and sisters,
about those who have died,
so that you may not grieve as others do
who have no hope.
For since we believe that Jesus died
and rose again, even so, through Jesus,
God will bring with him those who have died.
For this we declare to you
by the word of the Lord,
that we who are alive,
who are left until the coming of the Lord,
will by no means precede those
who have died.

Continued overleaf

For the Lord himself,
with a cry of command,
with the archangel's call
and with the sound of God's trumpet,
will descend from heaven,
and the dead in Christ will rise first.
Then we who are alive, who are left, will be
caught up in the clouds together with them
to meet the Lord in the air;
and so we will be with the Lord forever.
Therefore encourage one another
with these words.

Subject index

Commitment

Courage

Evening

Faith

Family

Help and healing

Humility

Journey of life

Joy and laughter

Kindness

Kingdom of God

Life

Living

Loneliness

Love

Mercy

Morning

Need

Patience

Peace

Quiet

Redemption

Rest

Righteousness

Sensitivity